Meet My Brother
General Junior

Written by Jennifer Lohr

Illustrated by Jessica Lohr

I dedicate this book to my own little Ambassadors and Generals, and everyone affected by autism. A very special thanks to my daughter for her illustrations - Abunnia is very proud of you, my Jes'! – Jennifer L.

I dedicate this book to my best friend, Gwen. – Jessica L.

Meet My Brother

General Junior

A Story About

Having a Sibling

With Autism

Written by Jennifer Lohr

Illustrated by Jessica Lohr

Hi! My name is Ambassador Alexandra,
but you can call me "Alex" for short.

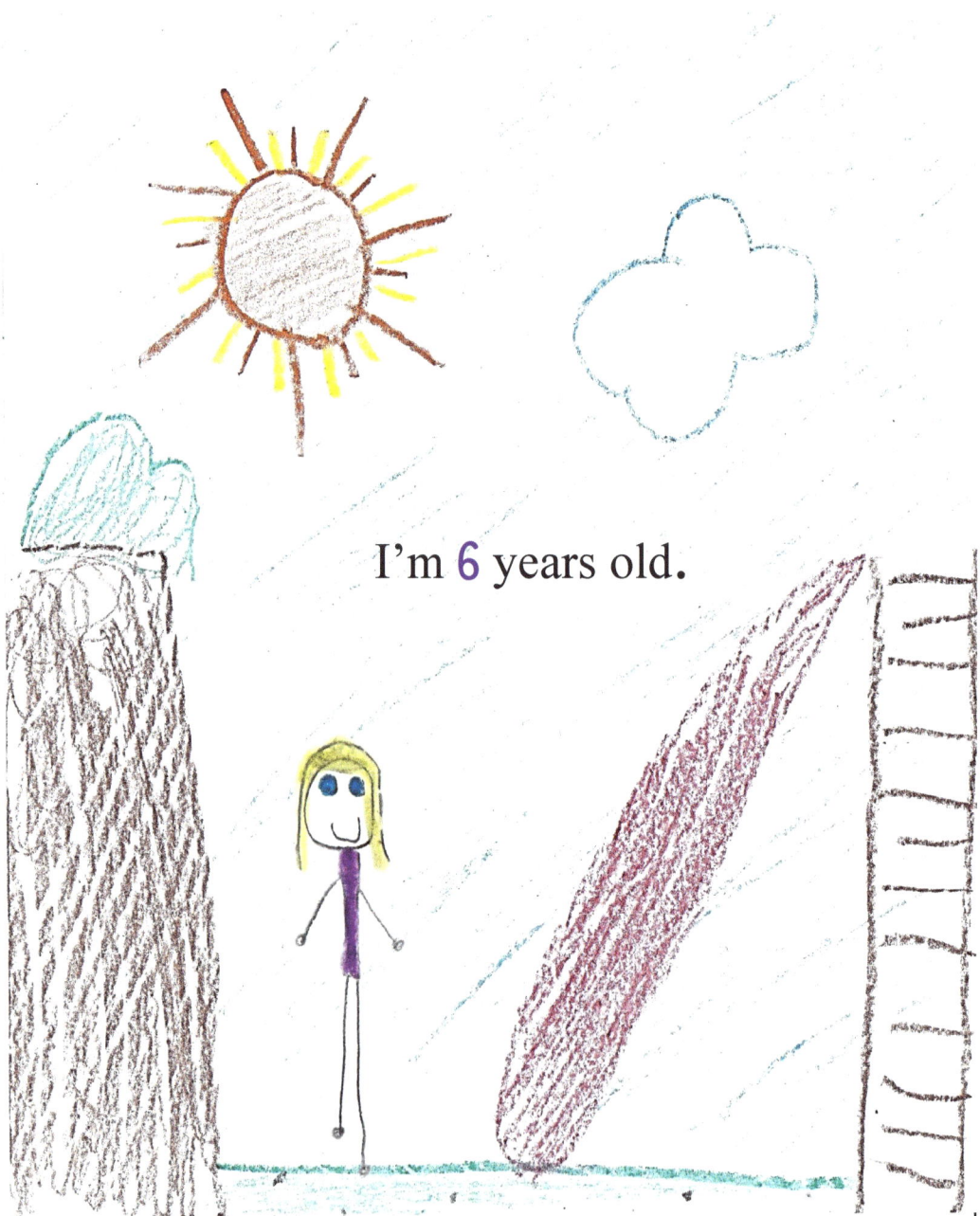

I'm 6 years old.

This is what I look like.

I am short and have **blue-ish** eyes.

Purple is my favorite color

I like to laugh a lot! I think knock-knock
jokes are really funny.

I live in a **yellow** house with
my Mommy and Daddy,
who are *really* old.

My Mommy just turned 30!

Daddy is even older than Mommy.
He says he is still young, but I'm convinced
he's really old, too.

I also have a big brother.

His name is Junior
but we call him

"General

Junior"

He is older than me and knows lots of

BIG words.

Actually, that is one of the reasons *why* he is
called General Junior …

…because he is really smart

and knows lots of

fancy

words.

Junior likes to tell people that he is

a decade

which is just a *fancy* of saying that he is

10

years old.

Our family also has a dog named Zappa.

Zappa is no ordinary pooch.

He does

TOP SECRET

kind of work.

He is called a

SERVICE DOG

I will even tell you a little secret:

Daddy says that "service dog"

is *really* CODE for:

SUPER HERO DOG!

Another reason why we call my brother

General

Junior

is because he has

autism

Just like he has **brown** eyes and a

BIG smile,

General Junior's autism is just a part of who he is.

My brother was born
with autism, but I wasn't.

Just so you know:
Autism is not
like the sniffles or sneezies
or anything like that.

You can't *catch* it.
You have to be born with it.

Having autism is not a bad thing,
it's just a *different* thing.

It's sort of like how we both have different

color hair.

My brother might do or say
things in his own little way, and
not like other kids.

That is just what makes him

unique

It's a fancy way of saying *special*.
Everyone is unique in their own way.

Some kids might not understand that my brother is
just being *unique*.

They might see him as different.

Some kids might not want to play with him.

General Junior doesn't usually seem to mind though.

Sometimes my brother just wants

to play by himself,

even if I'd like to play with him.

He can yell like he's angry.

He might run away from me.

I know it doesn't mean that I did

anything wrong or bad.

Mommy says that even though it *seems*
like he's mad at me, it's probably just because he's
"stimming."

Stimming is when too many
things happen all at once, and the General
just needs a break.

I kind of know what that feels like
because I like having breaks, too.

The General says that he feels very

overwhelmed or

stressed out when he needs a break.

When I need a break and want to play
    by myself, I have fun with my dollies.

I like to pretend they are General Junior

      and Ambassador Alexandra

on an adventure to

    save the world!

…or maybe just our neighborhood.

They are *always* the good guys, though.

Sometimes General Junior
will hear me calling my
dolly his name,

and I think he likes that.

One day General Junior was stimming and almost ran right outside, but Zappa blocked the door.

Zappa likes to help make sure that my brother stays safe.

It's just like Daddy said:

Zappa is a super hero dog.

When I see the General flapping his arms
up and down, I know it means he's very excited.

It's another kind of stimming.

He did that a lot last night when Granny
and Granpy came over for dinner, but they
knew he was just super glad to see them.

When we are out
shopping the General
can sometimes get worried
and might yell or cry.

Sometimes people will
stare at us.

I know not to feel sad about it
because he can't always help it.

Maybe he will learn not to feel bad about it, too.

My brother is still finding out how to feel safe around
other people,
but not everyone knows that about him.

One time at the store my brother shouted.

Then a lady told Mommy she was a

bad parent and that my brother just needed

"MORE DISCIPLINE!"

It was a little
scary.

I felt sad.

Mommy didn't
say anything and
we just left.

Mommy stayed quiet all the way home.

We talked about it later.

Mommy said she wanted to help more people understand autism.

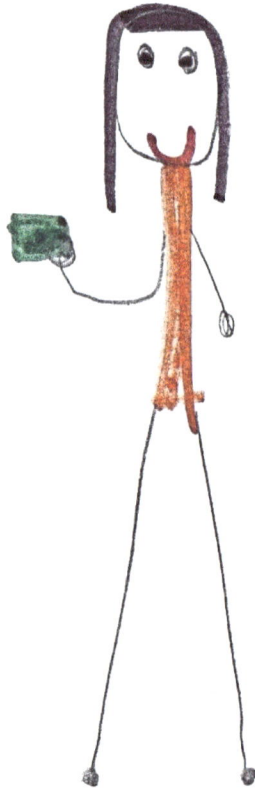

Since that day Mommy will give out little cards to people like that lady.

The cards tell all about what autism is.

People will thank her for the cards,

and for working so hard to

teach them about General Junior's autism.

Mommy says it's important to know things,

and that education is

POWERFUL

I wonder if we all get some sort of super

powers from learning new things?

I like going to school.

My teacher is Mr. Marshall.

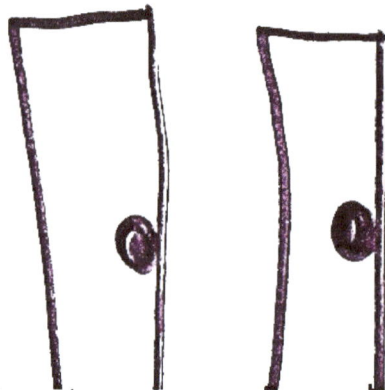

At school my brother's classroom has special helpers for him.

The helpers are called "aides."

They make sure General Junior has everything
he needs to help him learn the best,
even if it's a walk around the school
or maybe just a hug.

And I think they must be the best aides in the whole
world, because General Junior is

super smart

and gives very good hugs.

Sometimes Mommy or Daddy will take me for a special trip to the park

and it's just me and them.

We might even do silly things like race around the playground, or have a knock-knock joke contest.

I almost always win, by the way.

Once in a while Mommy or Daddy might have to

spend more time with General Junior than me.

I started to feel sort of left out

and I told my Daddy about it.

He said it was OK to feel that way,

and it gave him an idea.

So Daddy taught me a cool

SECRET

handshake

that only me and him know.

I like knowing Mommy and Daddy haven't

forgotten about me.

Mommy and Daddy tell me I'm still very important to them, no matter what.

Even though I don't have autism,

I like knowing I'm special, too.

I think being called
"Ambassador Alexandra" is pretty

AWESOME

In fact, did you know that the word

Ambassador

actually means someone who is very important?

I kind of feel really proud of myself for that.

My Mommy, Daddy, General
Junior, Zappa, Granny, Granpy,
and even my teachers all
fill my heart with
so much
love

And that makes me happy.

www.ingramcontent.com/pod-product-compliance
Lightning Source LLC
LaVergne TN
LVHW072112070426
835509LV00003B/125